THANK GOD FOR MY CROSS

CLARK CRAWFORD

FOREWORD BY DAVID ALLBRITTON

Copyright by Clark Crawford, 2010
All Rights Reserved
Published by
CrossHouse Publishing,
P.O. Box 461592
Garland, Texas 75046-1592
Printed in the United States of America
by Lightning Source, LaVergne, TN
Except where otherwise indicated, all Scripture taken from the Holy Bible,
New King James Version, copyright 1979 and 1980
by Thomas Nelson Publishers
Cover design by Dennis Davidson
Author photo by Lindsay Grant (972-302-6500)

ISBN 978-1-934749-94-4
Library of Congress 2010936950

Dedication

This book is dedicated to the One who made this book possible, Jesus Christ, who went willingly to the cross to take my penalty and the rest of the world's also. Nobody took His life; He went willingly and lovingly and laid down His life for me, so that I could be saved, write this book, and spend eternity with Him.

This book is also dedicated to the two greatest gifts in my life this side of heaven: my children, **Conner Crawford** and **Kelsey Crawford**. My life would not be the same without you. I am so proud of both of you. I look forward to spending the rest of my life loving and encouraging you.

Acknowledgements

As with any book, it takes a great team to make all of the elements work together. I want to extend my personal and sincere thanks to:

Ben and Rejoice Sarratt—You will never know this side of heaven how much you mean to me. You have been my support through it all. I love you both beyond words.

Jodie Brownd-Blancett—Author, Editor and Friend . . . I want to personally thank you for taking the time to help me make this book a reality. You are a Godsend into my life.

Gary Stevens—Thank you for constantly encouraging me when things seemed darkest. Your a God-send into my life, and if not for you, I would not be in the greatest church in America, The Winner's Edge - Garland, TX. God bless you my friend.

The Winner's Edge - Pastor David, Linda, and the church, I want to say "thank you" for receiving me and loving me unconditionally. This is the greatest church in America. The Word of God is preached with power, authority, anointing, and tears. The whole mission is to win the lost for Jesus Christ. Thank you for your years of faithfulness to our Lord and Savior.

Tracy Allen - I want to say thank you for the 30 years of love and support. Your a God-send into my life and ministry. May the Lord bless you exceedingly, abundantly above anything you could ever ask or think for your commitment to me and Jesus Christ.

My Intercessors—You keep me covered, protected and moving forward. I am forever grateful and blessed because of your prayers and support. Thank you.

Table of Contents

Foreword   13

Introduction   17

Chapter 1 The Cross   19

Chapter 2 The Denial   23

Chapter 3 Endure the Cross   27

Chapter 4 Forgiven Or Not   31

Chapter 5 Pain at the Cross   35

Chapter 6 Abandoned at the Cross   39

Chapter 7 Obedience Comes Through Suffering   43

Chapter 8 Time to Grow Up   47

Chapter 9 Demonstration of Love   51

Chapter 10 Glory in Tribulations   55

Chapter 11 Cross Times   59

Chapter 12 Sanctification   63

Chapter 13 Stop Rebuking, Start Loving   67

Chapter 14 The Blood Spill   71

Chapter 15 It's Time to Get Right With God   75

Chapter 16 Fear God   79

Chapter 17 Jesus Is Coming Soon   83

Chapter 18 Bless Him   87

Chapter 19 Fearfully and Wonderfully Made   91

Chapter 20 Finally I Am Crucified With Christ   95

Appendix: The Sinner's Prayer   99

I Want to Hear from You   101

Clark's Other Books   102

Foreword

This book is a reminder of the central theme of Christianity. Clark Crawford speaks from a lifetime of experience and motivates readers to search their hearts. This manuscript is filled with valuable Bible verses and insight to bring us all closer to Christ.

We live in an age of compromise and lukewarmness. Clark addresses these issues head on with Biblical correctness and Holy Spirit conviction. After reading it, I found myself desiring an even closer walk with God. Anyone who reads this book will find inspiration, conviction, information and motivation.

Clark not only speaks with a biblical mandate, but also through years of experience. He knows what it feels like to be lost, and he knows what it feels like to be found in Christ. Clark also knows what a half-hearted commitment is like compared to selling out completely to Christ.

Clark speaks with boldness, yet with compassion. He shows you the joy of following Jesus and victory in the Holy Spirit. You will also discover a soul-winner's heart and a man who has a burden for hurting humanity.

Every chapter of this anointed book explains the step by step process to total victory over every bondage in your life. You will discover great teaching on the blood of Christ, sanctification and common sense Christianity.

My wife, Linda, and I have grown to really love and respect Clark Crawford. He is a man after God's own heart. Being his pastor at The Winner's Edge Church, I can endorse him both as an evangelist and his personal character and walk with God. Clark is living out what he preaches. The work he has penned in this book will bless you and your family. Let me encourage you to get a few more copies to give out to your unsaved friends and even to dedicated Christians.

This books speaks to us all.

May God richly bless you and anoint your ears to comprehend the truth in these pages.

Your best days are yet ahead.

                              Sincerely in Christ,

                              Dr. David Allbritton
                              The Winner's Edge Church
                              Garland, TX

Introduction

On November 15, 2009, before going on my "Cross Times" radio program, the Lord said to me clearly, " Many people have gone to the cross, but did not die." WOW! It hit me like a ton of bricks. The Lord continued on, "They went there, but found it to be too painful. The suffering was too much for them. The Spirit is willing but the flesh is weak."

This encounter shed a whole new light on the cross for me. This is my message—but oh, how the anointing all of a sudden increased upon my messages.

This is the reason, that Evangelist Billy Graham stated many years ago, "that 60 to 65 percent of today's churchgoers are going straight to hell."

Friends, God is going to speak new revelation to you through this book. I believe that many of you reading it will find out as I did over the years, that I was lost and going to hell when I actually thought I was saved and headed to heaven.

Examine your heart as you read this book. I believe it is inspired by God. Make sure that you are saved and truly have your name written in The Lamb's Book of Life.

When God visited me at the radio station that day, I actually was in the process of writing another book titled "Unleashed".

It was clear to me that this book had to be written because of the multitudes of people who must hear a life-changing word so that they don't end up in The Lake of Fire—tormented and separated from a loving God Who says, "You must go to the cross and die."

Will you, on this day go to the cross, repent of your sins, surrender your life to Jesus Christ, and die to self, so that Jesus Christ can live in you and through you once and for all?

Chapter One

The Cross

Then He said to them all, "If anyone desires to come after Me, let him deny himself and take up his cross daily, and follow Me" (Luke 9:23).

The cross is a place of death. This is a place to which Jesus Christ went willingly for you and for me. To be crucified is the most horrible and painful death of all. If you read in Isaiah 53 you will see just some of the things that our Savior endured—all so that we might be saved. He was whipped, spit on, mocked, rejected and had nails driven through His hands and feet. While flesh fell from His body, a crown of thorns was placed upon His head as the blood poured out of Him. Oh, the blood! *What can wash away our sins? Nothing but the blood of Jesus. What can make us whole again? Nothing, but the blood of Jesus.*
    Friends, it started at the cross and it ends at the cross. Why is it that very few preach on the cross in this day and time? Why do preachers stray from preaching on sin? Why is it that preachers don't preach against homosexuality? Why is it that the world today calls good evil and evil good? I'll tell you why. They have no fear of God, the cross, nor the Savior who went there to bleed and die for a fallen world. It is time that men and women rise up and take their place in the "Army

of The Lord."

We must preach the cross, the blood, and the resurrection of Jesus Christ, the Holy One of Israel, Who defeated death, hell, and the grave when He arose from death on that third day. He then went to the lowest parts of the Earth and stripped Satan of the keys of the Kingdom and once and for all defeated him. Luke 10:19-20 says, *Behold, I give you the authority to trample on the serpents and scorpions, and over all of the power of the enemy and nothing shall by any means hurt you. Nevertheless, do not rejoice in this, that the spirits are subject to you, but rather rejoice because your names are written in heaven.* Have you gone to the cross and died, or did you go and find it to be too painful and then return to your same old ways? The definition of insanity is doing the same old thing over and over again, expecting different results. Will you agree with me that this is the day of salvation? Choose this day, Whom you will serve once and for all. To God be the glory!

Friends, the safest place on Earth is at the foot of the cross, humbled before God's throne. The more wicked the times, the more we need to stay yielded to Him.

If you want life—and life more abundantly—you must go to the cross and totally surrender your life to the One who died for you. His name is Jesus Christ, The Anointed One. It took me many years in the School of Hard Knocks to understand that it starts at the cross and it ends at the cross. Oh, the blood that was shed so that I could truly say, *I have been crucified with Christ; it is no longer I who live but Christ who lives in me.* The life, that I now live in the flesh, I live by faith in the Son of God, who loved me and gave Himself for me. (Gal. 2:20)

Prayer:
Dear Jesus, enter into my heart. The best I know how I repent of all of my sins. Please take my life once and for all and do as You will. I surrender my life to You; this moment in time I ask that You fill me with your Holy Spirit so that He can lead and guide me into all truth. Thank You for saving me now and writing my name in "The Lamb's Book of Life". In Jesus mighty Name. Amen.

Chapter 1 Scriptures to meditate on:

He that does not take up his cross and follow after Me, is not worthy of Me (Matthew 10:38).

He who finds his life will lose it and he who loses his life for my sake will find it (Matthew 10:39).

And whomever does not bear his cross and come after Me cannot be my disciple (Luke 14:24).

And being found in appearance as a man, He humbled Himself and became obedient to the point of death, even the death of the cross (Philippians 2:8).

Chapter 2

The Denial

Not everyone that says to me Lord, Lord shall enter the Kingdom of Heaven but He who does the will of my Father in Heaven. Many will say to me in that day Lord, Lord have we not prophesied in your name, cast out demons in your name, and done many wonders in your name? And I will declare to them, "I never knew you; depart from Me, you who practice lawlessness!" (Matt.7:21-23).

This should put the fear of God in you if there is any doubt that you are saved. Many people believe they are saved because they are a good person, treat people right, or have done good works. They believe that God would not send anyone to hell—and He doesn't. You and I send ourselves to hell when we do not accept His free gift of salvation. Again, it is a free gift. Ephesians 2:8-9 says, *For by grace you have been saved through faith, and that not of yourselves; it is the gift of God, not of works, lest anyone should boast.*

Friends, in Matthew 7:21-23 Jesus was talking to the religious. Religious people have rules and regulations you must follow. They try to run the church and then the pastor, instead of letting God and then the order that follows. They try to buy the pastor. They try to tell him what he can and cannot do. And when he doesn't do what they want, they vote him out.

Unbelievable, but I see this all of the time. This is a very sad thing, but God in His mercy is bringing judgment to the house of God in 2010. 1 Peter 4:17 says, *For the time has come for judgment to begin at the house of God; and if it begins with us first, what will be the end of those who do not obey the gospel of God?*

If you cannot tell, please understand and receive this word from the Lord, *"He will not always strive with us, Nor will He keep His anger forever."* (Psalm 103:9)

This book is a message that must be heard and I prophesy that it will reach every hand intended, in Jesus name.

If you are reading this book, you are either one of those religious people I mentioned,—surely lost and in need of a Savior, or think you are saved but are not, because you didn't die at the cross, or you are saved but God is giving you these instructions to share with family, friends, neighbors, co-workers and so forth. Do not take this warning lightly. You must share with the people with whom you come in contact. Spread the good news and do not let the blood of Jesus be upon your hands due to disobedience. You have what nobody else has. You can do what nobody else can do. You are the answer to the prayers of many other people. Go and do the work of an evangelist! We are all called to go into the world and preach the gospel. You are what the Word says you are. You have what the Word says you have. You can do what the Word says you can do. You are an over-comer by the blood of the Lamb.

Prayer:

Dear Jesus, please forgive me for failing You. Please forgive me for denying You and being selfish. I repent right now and I receive the blood to wash me white as snow. I am forgiven, saved, and baptized with fire this moment in Jesus name, Amen.

Chapter 2 Scriptures to meditate on:

Also I say to you, whomever confesses Me before men, Him the son of man, also will confess before the angels of God. But He who denies me before men will be denied before the angels of God (Luke 12:8-9).

Then He looked at them and said, "What then is this that is written: The stone that the builders rejected has become the chief cornerstone? Whomever falls on that stone will be broken; but on whomever it falls, it will grind to powder" (Luke 20:17-18).

Chapter 3

Endure The Cross

Looking unto Jesus, the author and finisher of our faith, who for the joy that was set before Him endured the cross, despising the shame and has sat down at the right hand of the throne of God (Hebrews 12:2).

Did you hear that? Who for the joy that was set before Him endured the cross. Glory to God! Jesus is our example. If we have been crucified with Him, then we can endure our cross daily. Is it painful? You bet it is! Is it worth it? You bet it is! I count it a joy to be able to suffer for my Lord and Savior. If you have read my last two books—*Thank God I Got Caught* and *Thank God For My Enemies*—you know that I know what it is to suffer. I know what it is to walk in the shoes of Job, David, Peter, Paul, Jeremiah and the other misfits that God turned around and used for His glory. He takes the foolish things of this world to confound the wise, and the weak to put to shame the mighty. I lost everything, denied Christ, sinned against Him. Yet God in His mercy caused me to have an encounter with Him that shook me to the very core and brought me to the cross. By the grace of God He spared me hell and set me free for His glory. Those great men and I now are touching the world with the truth of His gospel with the fire and anointing of Jesus Christ by the Holy Spirit. Only when you go to the cross and die to self and everything that the world has to offer will Christ fill you with Himself, kill every unrighteous thing in you, then sending you out humbled under the mighty hand of God to seek and to save that which is lost—fearlessly making known the mysteries of the Gospel in love and mercy, forgiving every person that has ever hurt you or will hurt you and saying the same words that Jesus said while bleeding on that old rugged cross: *Father forgive them for they know not what they are doing* (Luke 23:34).

Ask God to remove the scales from your eyes, so you can say, as Jesus said, *"For the joy that was set before Him, He endured the cross."* Joy is waiting to be found by all of you reading this book. On the other side of your wilderness is joy that is unspeakable and full of glory. There are people waiting to hear your testimony of how God brought you through your pain and suffering, set you free, gave you joy and now you are the answer to all of those people's prayers on the other side of that cross you have borne and carry daily. *In the world you will have tribulations; but be of good cheer, I have overcome the world* (John 16:33).

Our testimony must be, *"Live or die, I will serve Jesus Christ."* Are you a bondservant of the Holy One of Israel, or are you a lukewarm Christian, serving Him when things go well, but denying Him when things get tough? Remember this scripture, friends: *Jesus learned obedience by the things which He suffered* (Hebrews 5:8). It is when you are in the midst of the most difficult times in your life that you come to trust Him and know Him. When I was at the end of my rope, God has shown Himself to me in the most powerful ways. I love Psalm 40:1-3 where it says: *I waited patiently for the Lord; and He inclined to me, and heard my cry. He also brought me up out of a horrible pit, out of the miry clay and established my steps. He has put a new song in my mouth. Praise to our God for many will see it and fear and trust in the Lord.* Hallelujah to the Lamb of God!

Prayer:
Dear Heavenly Father, I ask you to help me see the joy that is set before me, so that I can endure my cross in a way that honors You and You alone. Thank You for setting me on fire with Your anointing, in Jesus Mighty Name. Amen!

Chapter 3 Scriptures to meditate on:

Therefore we also, since we are surrounded by such great a cloud of witnesses, let us lay aside every weight and the sin which so easily ensnares us and let us run with endurance the race that is set before us (Hebrews 12:1).

And let us not grow weary while doing good, for in due season we shall reap if we do not lose heart (Galatians 6:9).

Many are the afflictions of the righteous; But the Lord delivers him out of them all (Psalm 34:19).

Chapter 4

Forgiven Or Not

If we confess our sins, He is faithful and just to forgive us our sins and to cleanse us from all unrighteousness. If we say that we have not sinned, we make Him a liar and His word is not in us (1 John 1:9).

Friends, have you really been forgiven? Do you understand that when you confess your sin and truly repent, a change in character and a new way of doing things always will occur. True repentance brings brokenness, weeping, and crying out to God for breaking His heart. What was your motive for asking for forgiveness? Was it because you just flat out got caught and you did it out of guilt or shame; or because you had to satisfy someone else; or you didn't want to go to jail or prison? Or, was it that you realized that you hurt the Risen Savior Who died on a cross for you and paid your penalty? I hope and pray that from this moment on, you will have a reverent fear of God and never willfully sin against Him again.

If you are in sexual sin, adultery, illegal drugs, alcoholism, a gambling addiction, have a problem with pornography, had an abortion or are thinking of having one, attempted suicide or are thinking about it, have hate and unforgiveness or bitterness in your heart toward someone, I want you to call upon the name of Jesus Christ right now and give Him a chance. He really does love and care about you and the place you are in right now in your life. He is the answer to every hurt, pain, suffering, addiction, confusion, loneliness, suicidal thought, and so forth. Call out to Him. He has a great plan for your life. Nothing you have ever done or will ever do can ever separate you from His love. (Romans 8:38-39) For I am persuaded that neither death nor life, nor angels nor principalities, nor powers, nor things present nor things to come, nor height nor depth, nor any other created thing, shall be able to separate us from the love of God which is in Christ Jesus our Lord.

That is great news my friends. Let God hold you tight and tell you how you are the apple of His eyes (Zechariah 2:8). His thoughts toward you are great (Psalms 139:18) He loves you with an everlasting love. He just awaits your surrender just like that of the Prodigal Son. He went and wasted all of his possessions on sin—living like so many of us. Then he hit rock bottom and realized that his Father was the answer. He went home and found his Father waiting for him. His Father hugged him, kissed him, and gave him the best he had. His father did not say, "I told you so . . . you should have listened" . . .

No, he just loved him and was thankful to have his son home. That is a description of a Heavenly Father. He leaves the 99 saved to go after the one lost or hurting person. Is that you today?

Friends, I am living proof of God's unmerited favor, mercy, and grace. God knows how wretched I was and can be if I ever succumb to pride or self righteousness. We must continually humble ourselves under the mighty hand of God, and He will continually lift us up.

All we need to do is stay in the Word of God. Study David, Paul, Peter, Job and the other great men of God. They were the worst of the worst, yet God forgave them, changed them, anointed them, and the rest is history. God wants to do the same thing for you and me. What a mighty God we serve. Thank God for sending His Son to die for you and me. Because of Jesus, we can go boldly to God's throne, asking and receiving from our Father in faith all that we have need of—Glory to God!!! He rewards those who diligently seek Him.

Prayer:
Dear Jesus, Thank You for seeking me and saving me from hell. You are a friend that sticks closer than a brother. I repent of all of my sins. I believe that Your blood washes me white as snow right now. Amen.

Chapter 4 Scriptures to meditate on:

For God so loved the world that he gave His only begotten Son, that whoever believes in Him should not perish but have everlasting life (John 3:16).

For God did not send His Son into the world to condemn the world, but that the world through Him, might be saved (John 3:17).

If my people who are called by my name will humble themselves, and pray and seek my face, and turn from their wicked ways, then I will hear from heaven and will forgive their sin and heal their land (2 Chronicles 7:14).

Chapter 5

Pain at the Cross

He went a little further and fell on his face, and prayed, saying, "O my Father, if it is possible, let this cup pass from Me; nevertheless, not as I will, but as you will (Matthew 26:39).

Here is proof that Jesus Christ came down from heaven in the form of flesh. He was touched and tempted in every way that we are, yet without sin. Thank God for Jesus and His faithfulness to the Father.

Jesus suffered horribly and was rejected and hated just like many of us are today. When you take a stand for Christ, the world will do unto you what was done unto Jesus. John 15:20 says, *Remember the word that I said to you, "A servant is not greater than his master." If they persecuted me, they will also persecute you. If they kept my word, they will keep yours also.*

For many years I knew Christ, but I was not willing to die for Him. I would give Him certain things in my life, but I had idols that kept me bound and separated from His presence and blessings. Sure, He protected me from death, just like He did Job; the enemy can only do what God permits him to do, nothing more. But the consequences were painful beyond words. It is one thing to suffer for doing right as I know today, but when you have to suffer for sin whether it be pride, drugs, alcohol, hate, unforgiveness, bitterness, and so forth it is not worth it. Because of God's grace and mercy, I finally came out of the wilderness after 40-something years of hell on earth. But there are many that have died and gone to hell as a result of sin. Many could not bear the pain, so they blew their brains out or committed suicide in another way. Many have overdosed due to the pain, suffering, and depression caused by sin. The Bible says, *The wages of sin is death* (Romans 6:23). The Bible also says that if you sow to the flesh you will reap corruption (Galatians 6:8). Many are sick today as a result of sin. Many have lost their minds due to sin. The penalty is damnation, my friends, and the lake of fire (hell) awaits those who don't turn to Jesus Christ, repent, and make Him Lord and Savior of their lives.

I have such a burden to see people move out of darkness into His marvelous light. Friends, please listen to a man who went through things beyond description, but I am now alive, free, on fire for the Lord, in love with Jesus, and in love with people because of His grace and mercy only. No peace or joy exists apart from Jesus Christ being Lord of your life.

He is calling out your name today to the Father. He loves you so much. He wants to give you a new life of love, peace, joy, goodness, kindness, patience, and so much more. He wants you to be happy and blessed. Ask Jesus to help you, and He will come running. If you are reading this book today, then you need to know that God has not given up on you. The devil could have killed you if not for God having His hand on your life. You are in the right place at the right time, my friend.

God has a plan and purpose for your life, and it starts today. Romans 8:28 says, *"And we know that all things work together for good for those who love God, to those who are the called according to his purpose."*

Satan has tried to kill you and me time after time. The so-called religious crowds have rejected you and me and ridiculed us. At times even those that have supported us have left us abused and forsaken. But God will never allow us to be confounded before men. He will never allow us to be dismayed or put to shame before the world. What a mighty God we serve. To God be the glory for all He has done and is continuing to do in you and me.

Prayer:
Dear Jesus,
No longer will I push away the cup of suffering. With you, all things are possible. Give me Your power in place of my weakness and be glorified in all I do. Amen.

Chapter 5 Scriptures to Meditate On

My Brethren, count it all joy when you fall into various trials, knowing that the testing of your faith produces patience. But let patience have its perfect work, that you may be perfect and complete lacking nothing (James 1:2-4).

Beloved, do not think it strange concerning the fiery trial, which is to try you as though some strange thing happened to you; but rejoice to the extent that you partake of Christ's sufferings, that when his glory is revealed you may also be glad with exceeding joy (1 Peter 4:12, 13).

Chapter 6

Abandoned At The Cross

Then Jesus came with them to a place called Gethsemane and said to the disciples "Sit here while I go and pray over there." And he took with him Peter and the two sons of Zebedee, and He began to be sorrowful and deeply distressed. Then He said to them, "My soul is exceedingly sorrowful, even to death. Stay here and watch with Me (Matthew 26:36-38).

Friends, when you are at the cross dying to self, don't expect anybody to be there supporting you. That is sad but true.

Matthew 26 says Jesus was in great distress. He asked the disciples to pray. Matthew 26:40 says, *Then He came to the disciples and found them sleeping, and said to Peter, "What! Could you not watch with Me one hour?" Watch and pray, lest you enter into temptation. The spirit is willing, but the flesh is weak.* Right before this in the same chapter, Jesus predicted that Peter would deny Him three times. Matthew 26:35 says Peter said to Him, *"Even if I have to die with You, I will not deny you!"* Well, you know how the story goes. Many people in my life denied me as well. It is amazing that the closer you get to Christ, the further your friends get away from you. You must count the cost from the beginning. It will cost you everything to serve God, but the rewards are so awesome.

His presence is beyond anything this world could ever give you. This life of being His bondservant is the greatest life of all. Serving people and loving the hurting brings the greatest fulfillment. Now I know why God says it is more blessed to give than to receive. My greatest joy is when I see someone lost and hopeless hear the word of Jesus and receive His love through me. I delight when I see tears begin to pour out and, after giving their lives to Christ, they have the biggest smiles on their faces and give you the biggest "thank you's". I make sure God gets all the glory, but it is special to know that the God of the universe used me to save the person's soul from hell. To see someone's life changed before your face is wonderful. To see someone get off drugs, alcohol, pornography, stay married, repent of sexual immorality, see people forgive those who abused or molested them—well only God can do such a thing. But he uses people many, many times. Are you a willing vessel? Are you willing to count the cost and give your heart, mind, and body to Him for His glory.

There is not a greater decision you can make than to come clean from your sin and repent and turn to the Holy One of Israel, Jesus Christ. We are in the last days. Remember: God will never leave you or forsake you (Hebrews 13:5). Jesus is a friend that sticks closer than a brother (Proverbs 18:24).

If God is for you, then who can be against you? No weapon formed against you shall prosper, and every tongue that rises against you in judgment, you shall condemn. This is the heritage of the servants of the Lord and their righteousness is from Me says the Lord. What promises we have from the Word of God. You are what the Word says you are. You have what the Word says you have. You can do what the Word says you can do. Will you stand in agreement with me today on Psalms 119:11? *Your word I have hidden in my heart that I might not sin against you.* God will never abandon you. My prayer is that you never will abandon Him. He loves you so much and wants to have fellowship with you this moment in time. Stop what you are doing and take five minutes to tell Him how much you love Him and how thankful you are that He is your Father. Glory to God.

Prayer:
Dear Heavenly Father, Thank you for loving me when I was unlovable. When everyone else abandoned me, You were still there loving me and drawing me to You. Here I am, all yours! Amen!

Chapter 6 Scriptures To Meditate On:

But we have this treasure in earthen vessels, that the excellence of the power may be of God and not of us. We are hard-pressed on every side, yet not crushed; we are perplexed, but not in despair; persecuted, but not forsaken; struck down, but not destroyed – always carrying about in the body the dying of the Lord Jesus, that the life of Jesus also may be manifested in our body (2 Corinthians 4:7-10).

For we who live are always delivered to death for Jesus sake, that the life of Jesus also may be manifested in our mortal flesh. So then death is working in us, but life in you (2 Corinthians 4:11, 12).

Chapter 7

Obedience Comes Through Suffering

Though He was a Son, yet He learned obedience by things which He suffered (Hebrews 5:8).

Are you suffering at this time in your life? Are you going through a trial or tribulation at the moment? Are you being lied about or hated by anyone at this time? If you are, then I have great news for you. First, you are not alone, join the club. Secondly, rejoice for your reward is great in heaven. The Bible says in Matthew 5:11,12 *Blessed are you when they revile and persecute you and say all kinds of evil against you falsely for my sake. Rejoice and be exceedingly glad, for great is your reward in heaven, for so they persecuted the prophets who were before you.* You're in great company. The Bible is so awesome and full of power and truth. All we have to do is read it. It tells us what we are going to go through before we ever do. The truth is if Jesus went through it, then we are going to go through it. Hallelujah to the Lamb of God. To think that I am a threat to the enemy's kingdom is great news to me. I served the devil and evil for many years; no telling how many lives were shattered because of my past, but thanks be to God that I am now crucified with Christ, nevertheless I live, yet not I, but Christ in me (Galatians 2:20). As a result of dying at the cross and surrendering my life to Jesus, literally millions have been saved in the last year. Amazing what God can do with a nobody. I am now on television every Saturday night and on the radio every Sunday morning; thousands are getting saved through these two evangelistic outreaches. This does not include the churches I have preached at, radio interviews, and television interviews. Wow! And last but not least, I have written two books that are now touching the world and causing people to be radically saved. Glory to God. I tell you these things to give you hope. If God can turn my life around and bring about all these things in less than a year, then He can and will do the same for you. Just give up and say HELP!! God, through His Son, comes running and will clean you up, anoint you, and send you into the world to seek and to save that which is lost.

    With God all things are possible. You are an overcomer. Greater is He who is in you than he that is in the world. You can do all things through Christ who strengthens you. You're more than a conqueror through Christ who loves you.

    He chose you for such a time as this. This is the greatest hour to be a child and servant of the Most High God. The world is dying and going to hell. You are their answer. Do not wait another minute. Get right with God and dream big. Your greatest days are ahead. Nothing can stop you but you. Get out of the way and let God make your steps and plans sure. This is a new day and a new season in your life like you have never dreamed. You're awesome. You're a leader, so stop following and start leading. You may be the next Billy Graham, Benny Hinn, Paul, Peter, James, John, Jeremiah, Daniel, or the man after God's own heart, David. They were all a mess at one time, just like you and me, but they all became world shakers and world changers for Jesus Christ.

Hallelujah to the Lamb of God.

Prayer:
Dear Heavenly Father,
I ask you to make me a giant killer now through the cross and the blood in Jesus name. Amen!

Chapter 7 Scriptures To Meditate On:

For I consider that the sufferings of the present time are not worthy to be compared with the glory, which shall be revealed in us. For the earnest expectation of the creation eagerly awaits for the revealing of the sons of God (Roman 8:18, 19).

And we know that all things work together for good to those who love God, to those who are the called according to His purpose. For whom He foreknew, He also predestined to be conformed to the image of His Son, Jesus Christ (Romans 8:28, 29).

That I may know Him, and the power of His resurrection, and the fellowship of His sufferings, being conformed to His death (Philippians 3:10).

Chapter 8

Time to Grow Up

When I was a child, I spoke as a child, I understood as a child, I thought as a child; but when I became a man, I put away childish things (1 Cor. 13:11).

Friends, it is time to grow up and mature into the vessel God has called you to be. In this day and time, nobody wants to pay the price it costs for the anointing. It costs you everything. It will at times cost you your reputation. People will lie about you, hate you, curse you, mock you, leave you, gossip and sow discord about you, attack you any way they can. The truth is this: they hate the One in you. They hate Jesus Christ. They are the ones that hung Him on the cross and crucified Him. The devil has blinded the minds of people today and he is using anybody he can to try and destroy the work of Christ. Satan knows his time is short. He knows that he is going to spend eternity in hell fire; he is determined to take as many people with him as possible. I am determined to take millions off the path to hell and lead them onto the straight-and-narrow road to heaven. Not only that, but I am determined to see people have life and life more abundantly here on earth as long as they're here. I am determined to see divorce statistics go down, suicide statistics go down, and drug addicts and alcoholics set free in the name of Jesus. I am determined to see abortion statistics go down, the sick healed, the lame walk, and the blind see. Friends, God wants to put His Super on our natural. I prophecy that we are going to see the dead raised like never before and that signs and wonders will follow those who are totally dead to the flesh but alive by the Spirit of God. His Glory is about to be poured out in the earth today like never before.

God is raising up an army of warriors, and I am proud to be on the front line. Will you join me? Listen carefully, the attacks you are under this very moment are proof that the enemy believes you are capable of carrying out the call of God on your life. If the enemy believes in you, then it is foolish not to believe in the God in you. You're a threat to the enemy's kingdom—you are men and women of God. The trials and tribulations in your life are to test you and humble you, so God can see what is in your heart. Let Him mature you and prune you into the persons He has called you to be. Stop fighting God and yield to His work going on in you and your life right now. Everything is working together for your good. God makes no mistakes. He always knows what is best for you. He knows you better than you know yourself. He created you in His image. You are fearfully and wonderfully made. Marvelous are His works and your soul knows very well. Right this moment give Him your all and you will be forever grateful. I can assure you that you will never ever be the same.

Prayer:
Dear Jesus,
I totally surrender my all to you now. Perfect your work in me. I give you free reign. You bought me with Your blood. So I say, yes Lord. Yes Lord, yes, yes Lord. Amen!

Chapter 8 Scriptures To Meditate On

Not that I have already attained, or am already perfected; but I press on that I may lay hold of that for which Christ Jesus has also laid hold of me. Brethren, I do not count myself to have apprehended; but one thing I do, forgetting those things which are behind and reaching forward to those things which are ahead. I press toward the goal for the prize of the upward call of God in Christ Jesus (Philippians 3:12-14).

Do not remember the former things, nor consider the things of old. Behold, I will do a new thing. Now it shall spring forth. Shall you not know it? I will even make a road in the wilderness and rivers in the desert (Isaiah. 43:18, 19).

Chapter 9

Demonstration of Love

But God demonstrates His own love toward us, in that while we were still sinners, Christ died for us (Romans 5:8).

There is not a greater demonstration of love than what God did by sending His only begotten Son, Jesus Christ, to the earth to defeat the works of Satan, and then ultimately to the cross to die in our place. He died a horrible death in a body just like yours and mine. He was tempted and attacked just like you and me. He went through everything you and I do, yet He was perfect and sinless. Thank God for Jesus being willing to pay our penalty. Friends, that is unconditional love at its best. He loved you that much. If you were the only person on earth at that time, He still would have done it. Remember the scripture in Luke 15:4 where He leaves the 99 sheep to go after the one lost sheep. That was you and me. Wow!! The Lord is so awesome. Our finite minds are unable to understand this love fully, but daily I pray that He will allow me to see the depth, width, height, and length of this love for me. It is so unbelievable, yet true. Man, I want to know my Savior and Lord more deeply every day. How can you not love Him with all your heart, soul, mind, and strength? He is my all and all. He is the first person I think of each morning when I awake and the last person I think of when I go to bed. I just want to thank Him and bring glory to Him every day of my life. He has put a passion for the lost and hurting people in me. This consumes my mornings, days, and nights. I must save the world by doing my part, as well as by encouraging others to do their part, too. The world is dying and going to hell quickly. On a daily basis people are committing suicide and horrible crimes. Children are being molested, abused, and murdered daily. Children have no fathers, and that is the number one problem in America today. We must rise up and follow God and be fathers to the fatherless. We must become spiritual fathers to the youth and even adults in youth-detention centers, jails and prisons, as well as fathers to those still in the outside world before they end up there.

Please friends, fall on your face before your Heavenly Father this moment and repent of your sin and selfishness. We must ask God to fill us with the Holy Spirit and to empower us to go into the world and fight the good fight of faith. It is when you are weak that you are strong. When you are humble and broken, then God comes in and empowers you with His power and anointing to go change the world.

It is when you are totally dependent on Jesus Christ that you become the devil's worst nightmare. Step back a moment, pray, and then just listen for the still small voice of God to speak to you. He will lead you and guide you all the days of your life. His words, power, anointing, grace, and mercy enable you to be like Him. He gives you the words to speak. It is His voice within your voice. He changes you from the inside out. He will give you a new heart and a new mind. He gives you His thoughts and His ways, which will be all new to you. It is the greatest life—beyond anything you can ever ask or think (Eph. 3:20). You will do the impossible. Signs and wonders will follow you all the days of your life. The blessing of God will run you down and overtake you. The hand of God will be evident to all that He has you in His hand. Wow! You are what the word says you are. You have what the word says you have. You can do what the word says you can do.

Just pick up the word and begin to meditate on it day and night. You will become more like Him every day. Love, joy, peace, patience, kindness, goodness, faithfulness, gentleness, and self-control will be the fruit of your life. Can you imagine that?

Prayer:
Dear Jesus,
Thank you for demonstrating your love for me by dying on the Cross. May you give me the courage and strength to lay my life down for all those I will come in contact with from this day forward. In Your precious name I pray, Amen.

Chapter 9 Scripture To Meditate On

For God so loved the world that He gave His only begotten Son, that whoever believes in Him should not perish, but have everlasting life (John 3:16).

Love suffers long and is kind; love does not envy, love does not parade itself, is not puffed up; does not behave rudely, does not seek its own, is not provoked, thinks no evil; does not rejoice in iniquity, but rejoices in the truth; bears all things, believes all things, hopes all things, endures all things. Love never fails (1 Cor. 13:4-8).

There is no fear in love; but perfect love casts out fear, because fear involves torment. But he who fears has not been made perfect in love. We love Him because He first loved us (1 John 4:18, 19).

Chapter 10

Glory in Tribulations

And not only that, but we also glory in tribulations, knowing that tribulation produces perseverance; and perseverance, character; and character, hope. Now hope does not disappoint because the love of God has been poured out in our hearts by the Holy Spirit who was given to us (Romans 5:3-5).

In the last chapter we saw how God demonstrated His love toward us. In this chapter, we will see how tribulations perfect the love of God in us, along with perseverance, character, and hope. Friends, it is through the hard times that God perfects His characteristics in us. People want something for nothing. They are not willing to pay the price. The Spirit is willing, but our flesh is weak.

For years God would humble me and test me to see what was in my heart. Every time, until a year or so ago, I would turn to my old ways and habits. Then I would have to go all the way back around that mountain again. Suffering and pain due to sin. I love God, so don't get me wrong, but I was not willing to suffer and be broken for the sake of the gospel. The cross was too painful. This all goes back to the reason for me writing this book. For years I went to the cross, but I never died until just a year ago when I lost everything—and I mean everything. By the grace of God and only the grace of God,

He gave me the strength and courage to endure the cross. It was painful beyond words. I cried daily for six months or more. I repented of things I never knew were even there. I would weep and wail, and scream, and shout, and would sometimes be at the place of death in the natural. But God in His infinite mercy brought me up out of a horrible pit, out of the miry clay, and set my feet upon a rock, and established my steps. He has put a new song in my mouth – Praise to our God; many will see it and fear and will trust in the Lord (Psalms 40:2, 3).

Friends, I can tell you that I am not just a miracle, but I am a creative miracle. I was hopeless. Everyone had given up on me, including myself, but God, my Father, saw what He made many years ago, breathed upon me again and has done the impossible in the vessel. To God be the glory. Since I went to the cross and died a year or so ago, I walk in unconditional love, have peace that surpasses all understanding, have joy unspeakable and am full of glory; all the fruits of the Holy Spirit are evident in my life; all the hate, unforgiveness and bitterness are gone; and finally I have forgiven myself and all the people who have hurt me. In the last year I have published two books that are touching the world. I have my own Cross Times Television program and Cross Times Radio program. Only God could do such a thing. I could tell you so much more, but this book is not about me but about the Cross and Jesus Christ, my personal Lord and Savior. Hallelujah to the Lamb of God.

So remember, God is working in you to will and to do for His good pleasure. All the pain and suffering and tribulations are all a part of you becoming crucified with Christ; nevertheless, you live, yet not you, but Christ in you. Let Him do the work and you will be amazed at the miracle He works in you and through you. Do not fight Him, you will not win. Work with Him and you will be writing your own book telling the world what He and He alone has done in you and through you. I am proud of you, my friends, for allowing God to be God in you.

Prayer:
Dear Heavenly Father,
Thank you for giving me the courage to endure trials and tribulations. Thank you that you are conforming me into the image of Jesus, so that I will bring You glory in everything that I do in Jesus' mighty name. Amen.

Chapter 10 Scriptures To Meditate On:

Blessed is the man who endures temptation; for when he has been approved, he will receive the crown of life, which the Lord has promised to those who love Him (James 1:12).

For in Him we live and move and have our being (Acts 17:28).

Therefore let him who thinks he stands take heed lest he fail. No temptation has overtaken you except such as is common to man; but God is faithful, who will not allow you to be tempted beyond what you are able, but with the temptation will also make the way of escape, that you may be able to bear it (1 Cor. 10:12, 13).

Chapter 11

Cross Times

But Jesus looked at them and said to them, "With men this is impossible, but with God all things are possible" (Matthew 19:26).

The Lord God Almighty just gave me the go ahead to testify to what He and only He has done over the past one year of my life. Ever since I went back to the cross and totally died to Clark.

God is doing a quick work in these end times, my friend, as I am proof of that. Sixteen years ago I had all kinds of prophetic works spoken over me. Well, after 16 years, because of my disobedience, finally they are all coming to pass. It has been miracle after miracle. Door after door has opened. People continually come up to me and say, "Do you understand all that God has and is continuing to do in your life?" Seems like every week something great and new has happened, they say.

It is so overwhelming to me at times. I know it is God's grace that He does not allow me to get caught up in the moments. I must stay humble and broken before my Lord and God. The moment pride sets in, it would all go up in smoke. So I guard my heart with all diligence for out of it flows the issues of life. (Prov. 4:23)

I continually pray Psalm 139:23, 24, *Search me, O God, and know my heart; Try me, and know my thoughts; and see if there is any wicked way in me, and lead me in the way everlasting.*

Since losing everything one year ago and coming back to Dallas, TX, to start Clark Crawford Ministries, the following have happened:

• Written two books that have been published and are touching the world. (Remember, I did not know anything about writing books; I just had a dream.)

• Have been interviewed on different radio stations.

• Have been interviewed on different television stations.

• Have preached in churches.

• Have ministered to orphans and nursing homes.

• Ministered to Angel Houses throughout the Dallas area.

• Now have my own Cross Times Radio program on 100.7 FM the Word every Sunday morning at 8:30 a.m. CST.

• Now have my own Cross Times Television program every Saturday night at 8:30 p.m. CST on the Universal Access Network Ch. 34.

• Have been interviewed by a newspaper that reaches the Dallas-Ft. Worth areas and beyond.

• Hundreds of thousands of people, if not millions, have been saved.

With God all things are truly possible, my friends. We overcome the devil by the blood of the Lamb and the word of our testimony (Rev. 12:11). This is the only reason the Lord is allowing this testimony in His book. It is to ignite hope and dreams that have been dormant in you for years. Dream dreams and believe in the impossible. It is your time now to shine for Jesus. Give Him all the glory and He will do for you what He has done for me. God is not a respecter of persons. What he does for one child of His, He will do for another.

So pick up that pen and write your book. Go open that new ministry and believe in the impossible. Go to your pastor and ask him if you can do what you have always dreamed of doing. I am sure God has already gone before you and told him to say yes. Stop fearing and walk by faith. You must start doing what you can do, and then God will do what you cannot do. Your greatest days are ahead. Go now and let God fulfill all your dreams and vision, mighty man and woman of God.

Prayer:
Dear Jesus,
Thank You that with You all things are possible. Thank you that by Your grace I can deny myself, take up my Cross daily and follow You. I give You full control of my life from this day forward. In Your precious name I pray, Amen.

Chapter 11 Scriptures To Meditate On:

Now to Him who is able to do exceedingly abundantly above all that we ask or think, according to the power that works in us (Eph. 3:20).

For the Lord God is a sun and shield; The Lord will give grace and glory; no good thing will He withhold from those who walk uprightly (Psalm 84:11).

Delight yourself also in the Lord, and He shall give you the desires of your heart (Psalm 37:4).

Trust in the Lord with all your heart, and lean not on your own understanding; in all your ways acknowledge Him, and He shall direct your paths (Prov. 3:5, 6).

Chapter 12

Sanctification

But in a great house there are not only vessels of gold and silver, but also of wood and clay, some for honor and some for dishonor. Therefore if anyone cleanses himself from the latter, he will be a vessel for honor, sanctified and useful for the Master, prepared for every good work (2 Timothy 2:20, 21).

Friends, there is a process of sanctification after being crucified and dead to Christ. Once you have finally gone to the cross and died to self, then the process of sanctification takes place. This is a glorious yet painful process. Sometimes it seems like you're on a roller coaster from day to day. The process is never complete my friends. It continues till the day we pass from death to life. Hallelujah!

Romans 8:29-30 says, *For whom He foreknew, He also predestined to be conformed to the image of His Son, that He might be the firstborn among many brethren. Moreover, whom He predestined, these He also called; whom He called these He also justified, and whom He justified, these He also glorified.*

Do you see the process? We are continually being conformed into the image of Christ. It is all worth it. With God all things are possible. At this moment, you may look at the homeless man on the street as a no good, beat-up disgruntled misfit. But one day as God works in you by His Holy Spirit, you will cry and weep over this homeless man or woman. You will one day see them the way Jesus sees them. He died for them as much as He died for you and me. As a matter of fact, the Bible says that when you are good to one of the least of these, you are doing it unto Jesus. When you minister to the homeless, orphans, widows, prisoners, etc. . . . you have done it unto Jesus. There is nothing greater in God's eyes than loving the down and out. Clothing the naked and feeding the poor is at the top of Christ's list. Believe me, the Lord will take out your heart of stone, pride, religion, hate, unforgiveness, and bitterness. As the process starts, you will no longer love the drugs, alcohol, sexual immorality, gambling, etc.— you will begin to love being in church, being around the right people. You won't like rated R movies any longer, but you will begin to love what God loves, and hate what Got hates. You will walk like Jesus, talk like Jesus, act like Jesus, minister like Jesus, sing like Jesus, have love, joy, peace, patience, kindness, goodness, faithfulness, gentleness, and self-control like Jesus. Can you shout out loud right where you are? Can you say, "I am the redeemed of the Lord!" Can you sing, *"Let the poor say I am rich, let the weak say I am strong, because of what the Lord has done for us, give thanks!"* Hallelujah! What a life it is serving God and his people.

    I love the song, *"At the cross, at the cross, where I first saw the light, and the burden of my sins rolled away. It was there by faith I received my sight, and now I am happy all the days."* Wow! I just cannot get enough of Jesus Christ. The Holy Spirit is conforming you and me into the image of Christ this very moment. Shout unto the Lord a new song. Give Him praise, glory, and honor. We have so much to be thankful for. Our homes, cars, children, mates, water, electricity, health, etc. We will all have something to thank God for. This is part of the sanctification. Just always give Him thanks. You and I have so much to be thankful for. Our names are written in the Lamb's Book of Life. We are going to spend eternity in heaven where it is continued love, joy, peace—no more worrying or tears or fears, just worshipping God all the days of eternity. The sanctification process is well worth it. You will truly go from faith to faith and glory to glory.

What a great and mighty God we serve. To think He chose me still just blows me away. Open your heart and ask God to come in and start the process of conforming you into the image of His Son Jesus Christ.

Prayer:
Dear Heavenly Father,
I surrender my body, soul, and spirit to You once and for all. You are the potter, and I am the clay. Do as You will with me. I pray in Jesus name. Amen.

Chapter 12 Scripture To Meditate On:

Therefore humble yourselves under the mighty hand of God, that He may exalt you in due time, casting all your care upon Him, for He cares for you (1 Peter 5:6).

Come to Me, all you who labor and are heavy laden, and I will give you rest. Take My yoke upon you and leave from Me, for I am gentle and lowly in heart, and you will find rest for your souls. For My yoke is easy and My burden is light (Matthew 11:28-30).

And Joshua said to the people, "Sanctify yourselves, for tomorrow the Lord will do wonders among you" (Joshua 3:5).

Now may the God of peace Himself sanctify you completely; and may your whole spirit, soul, and body be preserved blameless at the coming of our Lord Jesus Christ. He who calls you is faithful, who also will do it (1 Thessalonians 5:23, 24).

Chapter 13

Stop Rebuking, Start Loving

Beloved, let us love one another, for love is of God; and everyone who loves is born of God and knows God. He who does not love does not know God, for God is love. In this the love of God was manifested toward us, that God has sent His only begotten Son into the world, that we might live through Him. In this is love, not that we loved God, but that He loved us and sent His Son to be the propitiation for our sins. Beloved, if God so loved us, we also ought to love one another (1 John 4:7-11).

For years I rebuked demons, the devil, and anything else I could rebuke. I yelled, screamed, cast down, cast out, and cast away everything that didn't live up to my theology or religion. After many years of living this way, I had a revelation from God by His Holy Spirit that changed my life forever and brought victory to me and my ministry. Friends, it is all about loving people, loving the homeless, drug addicts, strippers, bar owners, horse-track owners, Las Vegas owners, and every enemy. Love is what will never fail.

For years I would drive by a bar and say, "God destroy that place. I bind it in the name of Jesus." I have become very convicted of that just recently. The Holy Spirit spoke to me in a still small voice and said, "I want you to start blessing every person in that bar. I want you to pray for them and their families. I want you to love them and have the same compassion on them that your Heavenly Father had on you when you were spending your nights in the bars." Wow!! It hit me that God loves them as much as He loves me or anyone else. Jesus went to the cross and died for them. Many of those people are hurt, wounded, lonely, shamed just like I was. They are covering up their sins just like I did. Someone has to love them. They want to be loved because most never have been. They have been met by rules and regulations at church. They were judged before they ever even set down in the pews. Many will never even set foot back in a church, unless you and I go out and compel them to come back with unconditional love. Stop pushing the Bible down their throats. Stop loving in word and in tongue and start loving in deed and in truth. The hurting do not want to hear a sermon, but want to see a sermon in action. You may be the only Jesus they see, so stop judging and start loving. You have to catch a fish before you can clean it. We must love people to the cross. Many people, such as prostitutes, do not know how to dress for church, so let's get them there, disciple them, and teach them how to dress. Many people coming out of prison have to adjust to the free world. I know, because I was one of them. They need to be loved, discipled, and taught how to be a man of God, a father, a worker on a job site, etc. Let's love them, build their trust, and help them become all God has called them to be.

    Friends, there is only one way to accomplish loving and not rebuking everything in sight. It is to go to the cross and die to self, so Jesus Christ can come and live in you by His Holy Spirit. Then, and only then, can you have the fruit of Christ in you, through you, and all around you. Then you can be a light that shines in the darkness. Then you can love everybody, whether they are from the streets, gangs, addicts, enemies, etc. This love I am talking about in action destroys every enemy and causes you to defeat every demon from hell. Love never fails. The love demonstrated at the cross always overcomes every evil imaginable. Glory to God. You are lovable, teachable, sanctified, useful, and on fire for the living God—ready to destroy all works of darkness. Hallelujah to the Lamb of God. He is worthy to be praised. Stand up right now and give God praise for loving you and creating in you a clean heart. You're a new creation this moment; old things are passed away and all things have become new in your life. Go into your world and love the unlovely and watch love rebuke and destroy every demon from hell in Jesus name. Preach the cross, blood, and resurrection of Jesus until Christ returns. To God be the glory!

Prayer:
Dear Heavenly Father,
Fill me to overflowing with your unconditional love. Please bind every demon from hell that tries to invade or influence my life. Let Your love shine in and through me. Amen.!

Chapter 13 Scriptures To Meditate On

Let love be without hypocrisy. Abhor what is evil. Cling to what is good. Be kindly affectionate to one another with brotherly love, in honor giving preference to one another (Romans 12:9,10).

A new commandment I give to you, that you love one another as I have loved you, that you also love one another. By this all will know that you are my disciples, if you have love for one another (John 13:34, 35).

But I say to you, love your enemies, bless those who curse you, do good to those who hate you, and pray for those who spitefully use you and persecute you (Matthew 5:44).

Chapter 14

The Blood Spill

But if we walk in the light as He is in the light, we have fellowship with one another, and the blood of Jesus Christ His Son cleanses us from all sin (1 John 1:7).

What can wash away my sin? Nothing but the blood of Jesus. What can make me whole again? Nothing but the blood of Jesus. Revelation. 12:11 says, and they overcame him by the blood of the Lamb and by the word of their testimony, and they did not love their lives to the death.

Friends, there would never had been the remission of sins without the shedding of the blood of Jesus Christ at the cross. How could we not give our lives to Christ after what He did for us at the cross?

My prayer is that this book will bring you to your knees, and that you go back to the cross and die to everything that is keeping you from surrendering all to Jesus. It could be sports, drugs, alcohol, gambling, a girlfriend or boyfriend, hate, unforgiveness, bitterness, could even be your wife, husband, or children. Whatever you are putting before the Lord in your life needs to be put at the foot of the cross. You need to repent and let the precious blood of the Lamb wash you white as snow.

God will give you the desires of your heart, as long as you

put Him first. Give Him your mates and children, and He will come and make your family exceedingly abundantly above all that you can ever ask or think (Eph. 3:20). That is great news. Many of you reading this book need a miracle. You need to go back to the cross and repent of all your sins. You need to return to your first love, Jesus Christ. You need the resurrection power of Jesus Christ to raise you from the dead once you die. Then you can say what Paul said in 1 Cor. 2:2: *For I determined not to know anything among you except Jesus Christ and Him crucified.* Then you can stand on Philippians 3:10 where Paul said, *"That I may know Him and the power of His resurrection."*

Friends, the reason I am writing this book is because I lived through and had to suffer horrible consequences for not obeying what I am writing to you about. These truths come from real life experiences. But by the grace of God, I went to the cross and finally died to Clark so that the Lord by His Spirit could resurrect the very life of Jesus in me. Today I am crucified with Christ, nevertheless I live, yet not I but Christ in me. I am now an overcomer by the blood of the Lamb, and I am now qualified to write this book, so you too will overcome and be all God has called you to be. Remember, it all starts at the cross and it all ends at the cross.

Repent of your sins. Ask God to forgive you, and mean what you say. Let the tears flow and brokenness and humility come. Tears are healing. Let God do the surgery in your heart that needs to be done. Stop letting the devil lie to you. You're more than a conqueror. Greater is He who is in you than he that is in the world. You can do all things through Christ Jesus who strengthens you.

The wages of sin is death, but the free gift of God is eternal life in Christ Jesus. God formed you in your mother's womb before you were ever born. (Jer. 1:5) He has a plan for you and there is nobody that can do it like you. Rise up, take your place in the army of the Lord. Fight the good fight of faith, and stop looking back. Press toward the mark for the prize of the high calling of God in Christ Jesus. This is a new day and a new beginning for you. A family that prays together stays together. So start praying and continually give God all the glory and thanks for what He has done, is doing, and will do until His Son Jesus returns on that white horse with fire in His eyes to take back what belongs to Him. Glory to God!

Prayer:
Dear Jesus,
Thank you for willfully dying for me. Thank you for shedding your blood to wash away all my sin. I am so sorry for putting you on that cross, but from this day forward I will take back what belongs to my soul. In Jesus name. Amen!

Chapter 14 Scriptures to Meditate on:

In Him we have redemption through His blood, the forgiveness of sins according to the riches of His grace (Ephesians 1:7).

For this is My blood of the new covenant, which is shed for many for the remission of sins (Matthew 26:28).

And being in agony, He prayed more earnestly. Then His sweat became like great drops of blood falling down to the ground (Luke 22:44).

Chapter 15

It's Time To Get Right With God

Behold, now is the accepted time; behold, now is the day of salvation (2 Corinthians 6:2).

This chapter is for all who have backslidden from the Lord. Backsliding is a biblical term that means "falling away, turning away, apostasy." According to the apostle Paul, who wrote the verse above, *"Today is the day of mercy and grace."* In other words, if you ever plan to believe, that time is now.

Friends, this statement by Paul is both an invitation and a warning. The warning is as follows: Do not receive the grace of God in vain. Do not ignore, neglect or cast aside God's offer of mercy. Respond to it today, or you may never have another chance. Psalm 103:9 says, *"He will not always strive with us, nor will He keep His anger forever."*

Jesus warned that many believers would turn away and grow cold: *"Because iniquity shall abound, the love of many shall wax cold"* (Matthew 24:12). His message is clear: Many who have been on fire for the things of God are going to fall away.

Friends, it is time to fall at the foot of the cross and repent of coldness of heart. We are in the last days and you must not just go to the cross, but you must die there and let Jesus resurrect His life in you. All of the backsliding we see today – the turning away from faith to unbelief – comes at a time when you would least expect it. Rather, you would expect people to be drawing nearer to God. We are at the beginning of those days of "great sorrows" that Jesus referred to.

Even prominent voices in the world today agree: These are days of unspeakable wickedness, marked by uncontrollable greed, rampant sexual perversions, multitudes giving themselves over to addictions of all kinds, from drugs to alcohol to pornography. Some who have backslidden tell themselves, "I can get right with the Lord any time I choose. I'm just not ready. I'm not mad at God, I just need time with my friends, time to enjoy myself. I know God is loving and merciful. When I'm ready, I'll come to Him. I'll know when that time is." I hear these thoughts especially from the young people today. But remember what God said in Psalm 103:9. He will not always strive with you nor keep His anger forever. Is it really worth taking the chance? I don't think so! The Holy Spirit has compelled me to show you the danger of coldness. It is not that God turns aside from those who backslide; his grace is offered continuously. The blood of Christ toward sinners will never lose its power. But coldness has a powerful and predictable effect. Remember friends, I know because I lived through it to tell you these truths. You do not have to go through it if you will just hear the spirit of the Lord and obey.

The term "hardness" indicates a condition that is beyond the influence of any gracious pleadings, any persuading from the Holy Spirit. It begins with coldness – a self-imposed exclusion from God, with no intention of obeying the call of His gospel. For those who continue in coldness to God's voice —who keep distant from the Holy Spirit—hardness is the result. Hebrews offers this warning: *"Take heed, brethren, lest there be in any of you an evil heart of unbelief in departing from the living God. But exhort one another daily, while it is called today lest any of you be hardened through the deceitfulness of sin"* (Heb. 3:12-13).

Dear one, I exhort you right now, as Hebrews instructs, wherefore as the Holy Ghost saith, Today if ye will hear His voice, harden not your hearts, as (Israel did), in the day of temptation in the wilderness (Hebrews 3:7, 8). *"Let us hold fast our profession of faith"* (Heb. 4:14). God help us in these uncertain days to "take heed," lest any of us become hardened in heart in the day of our trial! You may think you could never harden your heart. But difficult times and trials are guaranteed to come to all who follow Jesus; no one is exempt. Therefore, *"Today, if you will hear His voice, do not harden your hearts"* (Heb. 4:7).

Prayer:
Father, open my eyes and heart to your truths and promises. Please don't allow me to harden my heart or become cold toward you. I repent of all sin and backsliding. In Jesus name. Amen!

Chapter 15 Scripture To Meditate On:

But know this, that if the master of the house had known what hour the thief would come, he would have watched and not allowed his house to be broken into. Therefore you also be ready, for the Son of Man is coming at an hour you do not expect (Luke 12:39, 40).

Watch therefore, for you know neither the day nor the hour in which the Son of Man is coming (Matthew 25:13).

Preach the word! Be ready in season and out of season. Convince, rebuke, exhort with all long suffering and teaching. For the time will come when they will not endure sound doctrine, but according to their own desires, because they have itching ears, they will heap up for themselves teachers, and they will turn their ears away from the truth and be turned aside to fables. But you be watchful in all things, endure afflictions, do the work of an evangelist, fulfill your ministry (2 Tim. 4:2-5).

Chapter 16

Fear God

Fear the Lord and depart from evil (Proverbs 3:7).

Here is the road to destruction: when there is no fear of God left in the land. Scripture speaks again and again of the fear of God: *"Fear the Lord, and depart from evil"* (Proverbs 3:7). *"By mercy and truth iniquity is purged: and by the fear of the Lord men depart from evil"* (Proverbs 16:6).

Listen to this story by David Wilkerson: "Years ago I was invited to speak at Yale University. When I arrived, I was warned that a group of demonstrators was in the audience ready to interrupt me on notice. As I stepped up to the podium, I saw some of those protesters holding signs. My message that night was, "Hell: what it's like and who is going there." I preached exactly what Jesus said, "There will be weeping, wailing, gnashing of teeth." As I spoke, there was total silence in the auditorium. The atmosphere grew heavy with conviction. Afterward, everyone filed out of the auditorium in stunned silence. I will never forget that service. There was a true fear of God in that place, a reverential awe even among those resistant to the gospel. A well-known writer for the New York Times covered the event. He later told me, 'The place was so quiet, my pen sounded loud.' As I walked through the lobby after the event, some of the protesters were still there with their signs. When they saw me, they turned away. They had no explanation for the majesty and holiness of God they had just encountered."

Friends, I tell you those days of godly fear are long gone. Today Satan has unleashed a gospel of convenience. David Wilkerson went on to say that there are now paid ads on New York City buses reading, "There is no God – Enjoy yourself!" On London buses, similar signs read, "There is no God – Let's party!" Why do such references to God persist over time? It is because humankind has never been able to fully shake off a fear of the consequences of sin. The world is nagged by the reality of a Judgment Day, a time of final accounting and a literal hell.

The Holy Spirit has been faithful to warn every generation, no matter how fallen. And He is speaking right now. If you are a pastor or minister of the gospel, I encourage you and warn you at the same time to preach the gospel with fire, anointing, and power that only comes from spending time with God. You must preach the cross, the blood, and the resurrection power of Jesus Christ. You must preach against sin, that hell is real, and that apart from a "relationship" with Jesus Christ, people are going there forever. *The wages of sin is death, but the free gift of God is eternal life* (Rom. 6:23). *If you sow to the flesh, you will of the flesh reap corruption* (Gal. 6:8). No more time for a watered down, tickle the ear gospel. People are dying and going to hell every day, while ministers candy coat the gospel, build bigger churches, increase programs that are producing no soul-winning deliverance from bondage, just a good ole time in the flesh. Stop fearing losing your sheep and being a man pleaser. It is time to fear God, or He will come and smite you just like He did Ananias and Sapphira. Stop quenching the Spirit. Get alone with God and let Him crucify you once and for all. Go to the cross, repent, and die so the Spirit of God can resurrect the power of Jesus and then you too can say, as Jeremiah the prophet did, "The word of God is like fire shut-up in my bones." You will not be able to contain it either.

Hallelujah to the Lamb of God. It is time to let God be God in you, through you, upon you, and all around you. Signs and wonders will now follow you all the days of your life, I prophecy in Jesus mighty name.

Prayer:
Dear Heavenly Father,
I ask you to give me that reverent fear of You. Thank You for convicting me of sin, righteousness, and judgment. I repent of all sin and I accept the blood of Jesus to wash me white as snow this moment. Amen!

Chapter 16 Scripture To Meditate On:

For God has not given us a spirit of fear, but of power and of love and of a sound mind (2 Tim 1:7).

There is no fear in love; but perfect love casts out fear because fear involves torment (1 John 4:18).

His delight is in the fear of the Lord (Isaiah 11:3).

The fear of the Lord leads to life, and he who has it will abide in satisfaction; He will not be visited with evil (Prov. 19:23).

Chapter 17

Jesus is Coming Soon

Then he said to them, "Nation will rise against nation, and kingdom against kingdom. And there will be great earthquakes in various places, and famines and pestilences; and there will be fearful sights and great signs from heaven. Then they will see the Son of Man coming in a cloud with power and great glory (Luke 21:10-11, 27).

All who believe in Jesus know in their hearts the time is close. Christ spoke much about it. It's true that no one knows the exact hour when He will return. Jesus Himself said as much. Yet He also described clearly the things that will happen just prior to His coming. "There will be wars and commotions, and many will come claiming to be Christ. But do not be terrified; the end is not yet." (Luke 21:8,9)

When will we see Him coming? Jesus says it will happen when "men's hearts (fail) them for fear, and for looking after those things which are coming on the earth: for the powers of heaven shall be shaken" (Luke 21:26). Some scholars say this passage refers to the destruction of Jerusalem in A.D. 70. But that couldn't be because the world at that time didn't see Christ coming in a cloud with power and great glory. The truth is this passage is one of the surest signals to us that Jesus is coming soon. Think of the shaking that's taking place today. The world is being shaken economically, morally, with natural disasters, with terrorism, with nuclear threats from rogue nations. What is the effect of this massive shaking? It is beyond doubt: People are more fearful than ever.

Amazingly, we don't hear much preaching about the coming of Jesus. Some preach that He will come but not in our time. Others preach, "The church has to take dominion first, and that could take thousands of years." (This belief is the foundation of what is known as dominion theology.) Jesus warns us about such thinking. He says, "But if that evil servant says in his heart, my master is delaying his coming." (Matthew 24:48) Paul echoes this: *"We shall be changed – in a moment, in the twinkling of an eye, at the last trumpet. For the trumpet will sound, and the dead will be raised incorruptible, and we shall be changed"* (1 Cor. 15:51, 52).

All of these passages speak of expectation. According to Paul, it is expectation that causes us to abound in the true works of God: *Therefore, my beloved brethren, be steadfast, immovable, always abounding in the work of the Lord, knowing that your labor is not in vain in the Lord* (1 Corinthians 15:58).

Jesus tells us very clearly: *"Be dressed in readiness, and keep your lamps burning…and be like men who are waiting for the return of their master… Blessed are those servants on alert when He comes. Blessed are those servants whom the Lord will find watching when He comes… And if He shall come in the second watch…you be ready: for the Son of Man is coming at an hour you do not expect Him* (Luke 12:36, 37, 39-40).

Friends, if this chapter doesn't give you a wake up call, then nothing will. Get up, be ready in season and out of season. Preach the gospel. Do the work of an evangelist. The harvest is great, but the laborers are few. We are in the last days. There is not much time left. No time to waste. Jesus is coming back for His bride. Are you ready? Do you have clean hands and a pure heart? Will He say, "Well done good and faithful servant?" Or will He say, "Depart from Me you worker of lawlessness, I never knew you." This should make you shake if there is any doubt that you're ready and surrendered to the great I AM. He is coming very, very soon.

Prayer:
Dear Heavenly Father,
Thank you for giving me wisdom to understand the times. Let me not be blinded or miss the coming of your Son Jesus. Fill me to overflow with your love, joy, and peace, and thank you for saving me in Jesus name. Amen!

Chapter 17 Scriptures To Meditate On:

"I am the Alpha and the Omega, the Beginning and the End," says the Lord, "Who is and who was and who is to come, the Almighty" (Revelation 1:8).

Nevertheless I have this against you, that you have left your first love. Remember therefore from where you have fallen; repent and do the first works, or else I will come to you quickly and remove your lamp stand from its place—unless you repent (Revelation 2:4-5).

Afterward the other virgins came also, saying, "Lord, Lord, open to us!" But He answered and said, "Assuredly, I say to you, I do not know you." Watch therefore, for you know neither the day nor the hour in which the Son of Man is coming (Matthew 25:11, 12).

Chapter 18

Bless Him

Bless the Lord O my soul; and all that is within me, bless His holy name! Bless the Lord, O my soul, and forget not all His benefits; Who forgives all your iniquities, who heals all your diseases, who redeems your life from destruction, who covers you with loving kindness and tender mercies, who satisfies your mouth with good things, so that your youth is renewed like the eagle's (Psalm 103:1-5).

Friends, we have so much to be thankful for. As I am finalizing this book, Thanksgiving 2009 is tomorrow. For many years I only thanked God this one day out of 365. The truth is we should live the other 364 days the same way we will tomorrow. If you are alive and reading this book, you have things to be thankful for. You're able to read, you have eyes to see, you are hearing the word of God. That is just the beginning. Do you have your health? Do you have electricity? Do you have water to shower in? Do you have food to eat, water to drink, a car to drive, a pillow to lay your head on tonight, covers to keep warm, a job, etc.? If you have any of these things, you are blessed and can be thankful.

The devil is a liar and deceiver. As a matter of fact, he is the father of lies. There is no truth in him. He comes to steal, kill, and destroy. (John 10:10) He hates you and your children. He is evil and wicked. He wants to destroy you and your children. Why would you want to serve him any longer? Hear me. He hates you, and he wants to kill you and your family.

Come out of darkness into His marvelous light. Repent of your sins. Ask God to set you free and heal your every hurt. Bless the Lord today. Bless His holy name. Remember from earlier in the book what (Psalm 103:9) says? He will not always strive with us, nor will He keep His anger forever. Right now, I can sense the war going on in your members (1 Peter 2:11). Beloved, I beg you as sojourners and pilgrims, abstain from fleshly lusts which war against the soul. Put on the mind of Christ. You must set your mind on the things above, not on things on the earth (Colossians 3:2). This is the only way to defeat the enemy. Think God thoughts, set your face like a flint on God, guard your heart with all diligence, for out of it flows the issues of life (Prov. 4:23). Put on the whole armor of God so you can stand against the schemes of the devil.

Ephesians 6:10-18 says Walk by faith and not by sight. Trust in the Lord with all your heart, and lean not on your own understanding, and He will direct your paths. Let the peace of God rule in your heart in every decision. If you do not have peace, then stop and pray, and then make your decisions. Be anxious for nothing but in all things by prayer and supplications. *With thanksgiving, let your requests be made known to God, and the peace of God, which surpasses all understanding, will guard your hearts and minds through Christ Jesus* (Phil. 4:6, 7).

This is the only way to live and overcome the enemy. Speak the word, believe the word, have faith in the word. It is how Jesus overcame the devil when He was tempted for 40 days in the wilderness by the devil. Whenever the enemy came at Jesus tempting Him, each time Jesus said, "It is written"...and the devil left him.

Jesus is our example. Follow Christ in all you do, and the enemy will leave you each time of temptation. Just say, "It is written." Speak the word of God for that circumstance, and glory to God, you will move forward to the next level. Can you say, *"Bless the Lord O my soul, and all that is within me, bless His holy name?"* O bless His holy name. Give Him praise and glory and honor. We are so blessed because of what Jesus did at the cross. He defeated death, hell, and the grave.

My prayer is that God resurrect His power in you, through you, and upon you. The same power that raised Jesus from the dead wants to raise you from the death you find yourself at. He is knocking on the door of your heart. Will you open the door and willingly let Him in? He longs to give you peace and rest. His mercy endures forever. His loving kindness is available to you this very moment. The Spirit of the Lord God is upon you this very moment. He is sending His power to heal your broken heart this very moment. He wants to give you freedom from depression. He wants to give you beauty for ashes, the oil of joy for mourning, the garment of praise for the spirit of heaviness: that you may be called a tree of righteousness, the planting of the Lord, that He may be glorified. (Is. 61:3)

I can see people coming to you and picking fruit from your tree. Surrender once and for all to the working of the Holy Spirit in your life, now in Jesus mighty name. You're awesome!

Prayer:
Dear Jesus,
I bless Your holy name. I give You all I am, and I ask You to come destroy all darkness within me. I ask You to

resurrect Your power in me, and that I walk, talk, and act like You the rest of my days. Amen.

Chapter 18 Scriptures To Meditate On:

I will bless the Lord at all times; His praise shall continually be in my mouth (Psalm 34:1).

Blessed be the Lord, who daily loads us with benefits, the God of our salvation! (Psalm 68:19).

The Lord bless you and keep you; the Lord make His face shine upon you and be gracious to you; the Lord lift up His countenance upon you and give you peace (Numbers 6:24-26).

And remember the words of the Lord Jesus, that He said, "It is more blessed to give than to receive" (Acts 20:35).

Chapter 19

Fearfully and Wonderfully Made

I will praise You, for I am fearfully and wonderfully made; marvelous are Your works, and that my soul knows very well (Psalm 139:14).

How do you see yourself? Do you see yourself through your eyes or God's eyes? Do you see yourself by your past or by God's word for your future? When you see yourself the way God sees you, all the doubt, fear, and unbelief will vanquish.

You see, God doesn't see you the way you see yourself. As a matter of fact, when you're a blood bought child of God, God sees Christ when He looks at you. The blood covers you and all your sins. Your life is no longer yours, but Christ who lives in you by His Spirit. So stop speaking death and let go of the past. Old things are passed away in your life and all things have become new. You are fearfully and wonderfully made by God, marvelous are His works, and that your soul shall know very well this day. Before you were ever even born, God formed you in your mother's womb and fashioned all your days before you. Yes, the good, the bad, and the ugly! It has and is continuing to work together for your good, if you love God. (Rom. 8:28) Do you love God? If so, then you can stand on the promises of God. They are yes and Amen! God cannot lie. Jeremiah 29:11 says, *"For I know the thoughts that I think toward you, says the Lord, thoughts of peace and not of evil, to give you a future and a hope."*

You're a king's kid. You're a royal priesthood and a chosen generation. If God is for you, then who can be against you? You must be awful special for Christ to die for you. He shed His blood and took your penalty at The Cross. He had nails driven through His hands for you. He had nails driven through His feet for you. He bled and died a horrible death for you. He even spoke to you from the cross. While you and I were in our deepest, darkest, and hidden sin, He said, "Father, forgive them because they don't know what they are doing." Hurting people hurt people. I was one hurting person for many years, and I know many of you reading this book right now are hurting very bad. Some of you don't even want to live another day. You have given up, you're suicidal, you want to put another needle in your arm, or maybe take another drink hoping that you will go to sleep and not wake up. Many of you are on prescription drugs for depression, oppression, fear, bipolar, etc. But God can and will heal your broken heart this very moment if you will just cry out, "Help! God, I don't want to live another day, but I know that it is not just coincidence that I am reading this book this very moment. I believe that if you can heal this man writing this book, then you can heal me. So I repent of all my sin. I ask you to do for me what I cannot do. I acknowledge that I have sinned and that I need a savior. Please save me right now and fill me with your Holy Spirit. I give up finally, and I now ask You to take my life and do what you please."

Friends, if you said those words and really meant it, then you can expect a drastic change in the way you think, talk, act, walk, etc. Read the Word of God, even when you don't understand it. Ask the Holy Spirit to teach you the Word. Ask Him to make the Word of God alive. I promise you, He will! You are today what the Word of God says you are. You have today what the Word of God says you have. You can do today what the Word says you can do.

Have faith in God. *Now faith is the substance of things hoped for, the evidence of things not seen.* (Hebrews 11:1) You must speak your future into existence. You must see it before you will have it. Trust God with all your heart. He is working in your heart, mind, and life right this moment. You may not understand it, but that is where faith comes in. Do not doubt, but believe, and you will have your dreams, visions, and desires mighty man and woman of God. This is the first day of the rest of your life. You're a giant killer, just like David was. When you're in the fire like Shadrach, Meshach, and Abed-Nego. God is there with you. When you're in the lions den like Daniel, God is there with you. With God all things are possible and nothing shall be impossible. Do you believe? If so, get ready for the third great awakening. You're a part of destiny.

Prayer:
Dear Jesus,
I believe you're the Son of God. I believe that I am fearfully and wonderfully made; marvelous are Your works; and that my soul knows very well. Fill me, lead me, guide me, and teach me all the days of my life, starting right now. I confess that I walk by faith and not by sight in Your Holy name. Amen.

Chapter 19 Scriptures To Meditate On

Now faith is the substance of things hoped for, the evidence of things not seen (Hebrews 11:1).

I will praise You, for I am fearfully and wonderfully made; marvelous are your works; and that my soul knows very well (Psalm 139:14).

My frame was not hidden from You, when I was made in secret, and skillfully wrought in the lowest parts of the earth. Your eyes saw my substance, being yet unformed. And in your book they all were written, the days fashioned for me, when as yet there were none of them (Psalm 139:15,16).

For I know the thoughts that I think toward you, says the Lord, thoughts of peace and not of evil, to give you a future and a hope (Jeremiah 29:11).

Chapter 20

Finally I am Crucified With Christ

I have been crucified with Christ; it is no longer I who live, but Christ lives in me; and the life which I now live in the flesh I live by faith in the Son of God, who loved me and gave Himself for me (Gal. 2:20).

Here we are at the end of another book. At the beginning I told you that God had showed me a few weeks ago that many people have gone to the cross, but they did not die. This last chapter's title is what I pray all of you are able to speak and mean this day in Jesus name. You must die to self. You must be crucified with Christ. It is not enough just to go to the cross, but you must be broken and brought to the end of yourself. It can only happen when you surrender your life, dreams, visions, mate, children, cars, homes, and idols to Him, Jesus Christ, who bought you with His blood. This is the greatest demonstration of love that has ever been shown. Who for the joy that was set before Him (Jesus) endured the cross; despising the shame, and has sat down at the right hand of the throne of God.

Friends, let this day be the end of your life; that Christ may once and for all take over residence in your body. Can you speak (1 Cor. 6:19) and mean it? Do you know that your body is the temple of the Holy Spirit who is in you, whom you have from God, and you are not your own? Your greatest days are ahead. This is the first day of the rest of your life. You will never be the same, nor your mates, nor your children, nor your church, nor your work place, nor your new business, nor your new ministry. Hallelujah! You have finally been crucified with Christ. Finally, you have not only gone to the cross, but you died! Glory to God!

You are now a light in every dark place. You are now recognized everywhere you go. When you walk into a room, the whole atmosphere changes. When you walk into a room, I can hear people already saying, "That is a man of God or that is a woman of God." That hate you once had, say goodbye to it. That bitterness that was once rooted in you and defiled many, say goodbye, and hear the words of your heavenly Father this minute, "You are forgiven." How about your best friend, fear? Well, he died at the cross with you. Say goodbye to fear once and for all.

Now, welcome your best friends into your new home. Meet love, joy, peace, patience, kindness, goodness, faithfulness, and self-control. They will never leave you or forsake you as long as you deny yourself, take up your cross daily and follow Jesus. Remember, without faith it is impossible to please Him. (Heb. 11:6) Walk hand in hand with faith. The greatest gift of all, though, is love because faith and every other gift works by love. Without love you and I are nothing. And remember to love your enemies, bless those who curse you, do good to those who hate you, and pray for those who spitefully use you and persecute you. (Matt. 5:44) This is only possible when you have gone to the cross and died once and for all. Isn't this the greatest love story of all?

This is almost like a fairy tale, but I know it to be true.

You see, a year ago, after many years of going to the cross, I finally not only went there, but by the grace of God, in a jail cell of all places, I finally surrendered my life to Jesus and died there. The benefits have been exceedingly, abundantly above anything I could have ever asked or thought. (Eph. 3:20) With men this is impossible, but with God all things are possible. You see, I lived that, too. Please hear my story and learn from it, my friends. You see, I am like Paul and Joseph; I went to prison. Like Peter, too, denied Christ. Oh yes David and I had a lot in common too, but thanks be to God, he says over me what he said over David, "Clark is a man after My own heart." I also am a little like Jeremiah. I can say, "The word of God is like fire shut up in my bones." And well, Job and I had a lot in common. I, too, lost everything, yet by the grace of God, I have overcome and mine is on the way back as I write this book. The last chapter of my life story is yet to be written.

I tell you all these things that you might know. I have gone before you and paid the price, so that if you will hear the voice of the Lord off these pages, and heed His every instruction, you will not have to suffer all the hell I went through. Yes, there will still be suffering and pain, but you will have the strength and courage to overcome. You won't have to go to jail, prison, insane, hell, divorce court, AANA anymore, just soak in the presence of God and let Him take you places you never even dreamed of.

Dream dreamers and believe in the impossible. Signs and wonders are now going to follow you everywhere you go. The blessings of God are running you down and overtaking you. You have gone to the cross and died. Now you shall live a life that pleases God and brings great glory to Jesus Christ. I love you, and I am so proud of you. See you in heaven!!

Prayer:
Dear Heavenly Father,
Thank you that I am crucified with Your Son Jesus, yet I live to give You glory in all I do. Amen!

Chapter 20 Scriptures to Meditate On:

I have been crucified with Christ; it is no longer I who live, but Christ lives in me; and the life which I now live in the flesh I live by faith in the Son of God, who loved me and gave Himself for me (Gal. 2:20).

But the fruit of the Spirit is love, joy, peace, patience, kindness, goodness, faithfulness, gentleness, self-control. Against such there is no law (Gal. 5:22-23).

And let us not grow weary while doing good, for in due season we shall reap if we do not lose heart (Gal. 6:9).

Surely goodness and mercy shall follow me all the days of my life, and I will dwell in the house of the Lord forever (Psalm 23:6).

Appendix

The Sinner's Prayer

The Bible says, *"God so loved the world that He gave his only Son, that whoever believes in Him shall not perish but have everlasting life"* (John 3:16). All of us have done, said, or thought things that are wrong. This is called sin.

Our sins have separated us from God. The Bible says, *"All have sinned and fall short of the glory of God"* (Romans 3:23). God is perfect and holy, and our sins separate us from God forever. The Bible says, *"The wages of sin is death, but the gift of God is eternal life through Jesus Christ our Lord"* (Romans 6:23).

God sent his only Son, Jesus Christ, to die for our sins. Jesus is the Son of God. He lived a sinless life and then died on the cross to pay the penalty for our sins. *"God demonstrates how his own love for us in that while were yet sinners Christ dies for us"* (Romans 5:8). Jesus rose from the dead and now He lives in Heaven with God His Father. He offers us the gift of eternal life-of living forever with Him in Heaven if we accept Him as our Lord and Savior. Jesus, said, *"I am the way and the truth and the life. No one comes to the Father accept by me"* (John 14:6).

God reaches out in love to you and wants you to be His child. *"As many as received Him, to them gave the right to become children of God, only to those who believe in His name"* (John 1:12).

You can choose to ask Jesus Christ to forgive you of your sins and come into your life as your Lord and Savior. If you want to accept Christ as your Savior and turn from your sins, you can ask Him to be your Savior by praying a prayer like this:

"Lord Jesus, I believe you are the son of God. Thank You for dying on the cross for my sins. Please forgive my sins and give me the gift of eternal life. I ask You into my life and heart to be my Lord and Savior. I want to serve You always." Amen.

Did you pray this prayer? If so, please contact me and I will be glad to assist you in your new walk with Jesus.

I WANT TO HEAR FROM YOU!

    Beloved, if you have prayed that simple prayer, I believe you have been born again. Your name has been written in the Lamb's Book of Life in Heaven. You will spend eternity with God. This is the greatest decision you have ever made.

    I encourage you to get involved in a Bible-based church and keep God in first place in your life.

    I love you and will be praying for you.

    I also would love to hear from you!

    To contact me, write to:

Clark Crawford Ministries
P.O. Box 570131
Dallas, Texas 75357
214-306-3061
Email:clark@clarkcrawfordministries.com
Website:www.clarkcrawfordministries.com

Enjoy Clark's other books

Thank God I Got Caught- From Prisoner to Worshiper:
Thank God I got caught with 10,000 hits of ecstasy and $40,000 cash on September 23, 1988. Clark Crawford was convicted of "conspiracy to possess a controlled substance" on January 12, 1990, and was given 20 years in the Texas Department of Corrections (Prison). Clark was devastated since the judge had told him that he would get 10 years "deferred adjudicated probation." All Clark could remember is his mother screaming out in the courtroom as the sentence was read and he was taken away.

Find out why 20 years later Clark wrote, *Thank God I Got Caught- From Prisoner To Worshipper*.

Thank God For My Enemies:
Clark Crawford has been reduced to love because of his enemies and has learned the real meaning of forgiveness because of some recent events by those whom he thought loved him. In Genesis 15:20, Joseph said to his brothers, (who sold him into slavery, *"But as for you, you meant it for evil against me; but God meant it for good, in order to bring it about as it is on this day, to save many people alive."* Clark has learned firsthand, but I say to you, love your enemies, bless those who curse you, do good to those who hate you, and pray for those who spitefully use you and persecute you (Matthew 5:44). You will look at your enemies in a whole different light after reading this power packed book inspired by God.

See order information on next page

All three of Clark's books are available by ordering on the internet at *www.hannibalbooks.com, www.amazon.com, www.barnesandnoble.com*, and at other online and physical bookstores as well as Clark's own website:

www.clarkcrawfordministries.com

You can also contact us by phone and we will be glad to send you a copy.

www.ingramcontent.com/pod-product-compliance
Lightning Source LLC
Chambersburg PA
CBHW052105070526
44584CB00017B/2339